Lizzy's Day at the Zoo

Story by
Mitchell Page

Lizzy's Day at the Zoo
Copyright © Mitchell Page
First published 2022 - Updated July 2025
ISBN: 978-1-7640294-5-2

All rights reserved. Without limiting the rights under copyright reserved above, no part of this publication may be reproduced, stored in or introduced into a database and retrieval system or transmitted in any form or by any means (electronic, mechanical, photocopying, recording or otherwise) without the prior written permission of the owner of the copyright.

Original illustrations/ Photographs by Samantha Zaleski

For Elizabeth

Today Lizzy is going to the zoo with her family.
"Come on Dad
Hurry up Daddy
It's time to go to the zoo!"
They all rush out the door……..
But, not before they get their sunscreen!

When everyone is in the car, Daddy says:
"Remember to buckle up!"
Click click go the seat belts
"We're going to the zoo!
We're going to the zoo!
Da da da da da da we're going to the zoo!"
Lizzy shouts.

When they all arrive at the big gates,
Dad buys the tickets.
"Three tickets, please"
he says to the lady behind the counter.

As soon as they enter the gates,
they are greeted by lots of kangaroos
jumping all around them.
"Look Dad!! Look look!!
They have very big feet" Lizzy says.
"That is so they can go bounce bounce bounce
all day long" says Daddy.

They then move on to see the monkeys.
"Oo oo ah ah" Lizzy cries,
pretending to be a monkey.
She loves hearing the monkeys talk to each other.
Like her, they can get very, very noisy.

Next, they see the giraffes.
"Look at their loooooooong necks!" Lizzy says.
She stretches her arm up and up as high as she can,
pretending that she has a giraffe's neck.

After that, they go to see the elephants.
"They have looong trunks that go brrrrr"
Lizzy then swings her arm from side to side pretending that it is a long trunk.

Lastly, they stop to see the lion.
"RAWRRRR!" Lizzy yells.
"I'm a lion and I like to eat and roar!"
This makes both Dad and Daddy laugh very much.

Before they go home,
everyone sits down for ice cream.
"Did you have a fun day?" Dad asks Lizzy.
"YES" shouts Lizzy, "I hope we come back soon!"

www.ingramcontent.com/pod-product-compliance
Lightning Source LLC
Chambersburg PA
CBHW040320100526

44583CB00004BB/166